AS １

The Ph

Barry Crump

Hodder Moa Beckett

ISBN 1-86958-354-X

© 1996 Barry Crump

Published in 1996 by Hodder Moa Beckett Publishers Limited
[a member of the Hodder Headline Group]
4 Whetu Place, Mairangi Bay, Auckland, New Zealand

Typeset by TTS Jazz, Auckland

Printed through Bookbuilders

All rights reserved. No part of this publication may be
reproduced or transmitted in any form or by any means,
electronic or mechanical, including photocopying, recording,
or any information storage and retrieval system, without
permission in writing from the publisher.

AS THE SAYING GOES

Every now and again we come across a description
or a truth that tickles our fancy, as these ones
have tickled mine. I've picked them up or I've
thought them up over the years and I offer them
here in the hope that they'll entertain you
or amuse you or put the thought together
for you, as they've done for me.

Some of them might even tickle your fancy,
as the saying goes.

Crumpy

AS THE SAYING GOES

You can do anything you like in this life as long as it doesn't interfere with anyone else's trip.

AS THE SAYING GOES

All I require of a friend is that their heart's in the right place.

AS THE SAYING GOES

Wouldn't it be a dull old world if all the flowers in the garden were the same shape and colour.

Bahai

AS THE SAYING GOES

I've never heard a middle-aged or old person say that physical punishment or hard work did them any harm when they were kids.

AS THE SAYING GOES

Sex and money have one thing in common, the more you get the more you get, and the less you get the less you get.

AS THE SAYING GOES

Don't hunt for deer in pig country.

AS THE SAYING GOES

A good thing taken to excess is worse than if you never had it at all.

AS THE SAYING GOES

Some of the greatest nitwits I've met have been academics.

AS THE SAYING GOES

Loneliness is all it's cracked up to be.

AS THE SAYING GOES

Words like "got to", "have to", "ought to", "must", "should", could all be dropped in favour of "need to be able to".

AS THE SAYING GOES

THINGS I CAN'T FIGURE OUT

How come they call rain bad weather?

With all the unwanted children

how come it's so difficult to adopt one?

AS THE SAYING GOES

How come they can immediately find vast
sums of money for war or to cover some
bureaucratic ballsup but none for the
parent whose little boy or girl needs
a bone marrow transplant?

continued . . .

AS THE SAYING GOES

How come doctors still use the
Hippocratic Oath?

How come people who plead Not Guilty
in court and are found to be Guilty
aren't charged with perjury?

AS THE SAYING GOES

How come lawyers?

How come the tax collector has more
power than the police?

How come individuals can get
and squander millions?

AS THE SAYING GOES

The quickest bit of legislation I ever knew to go through parliament was when both sides of the House voted themselves a big retrospective pay rise.

AS THE SAYING GOES

If you've got a boring task to do, do it the very best you possibly can and it will cease to be boring.

AS THE SAYING GOES

I'd rather be offered a reason than an excuse.

AS THE SAYING GOES

Keep your head down and your strides on and your mouth shut and weave your way through life.

AS THE SAYING GOES

Anyone who keeps a savage dog
is scared of something.

AS THE SAYING GOES

Cruelty to animals is a horrible crime.

AS THE SAYING GOES

In this day it's not enough to do unto others as you would be done by. Prefer your brother to yourself if you care about peace and harmony.

Bahai

AS THE SAYING GOES

Prejudice is a bloody drag.

AS THE SAYING GOES

We should do everything as though we were being watched by our best friend, because we are.

AS THE SAYING GOES

People who punish your ear with religion
are wasting your time and theirs.

AS THE SAYING GOES

 $\mathbf{I}$ tried to find out what they mean by inflation and discovered that they were talking about plain old greed.

AS THE SAYING GOES

Spare the rod or your kids'll charge you with assault.

AS THE SAYING GOES

N̲o one ever got anything for nothing
that was any real use to them.

AS THE SAYING GOES

Once we establish exactly what a problem is, the solution becomes obvious.

AS THE SAYING GOES

I've never known anyone who was all good or anyone who was all bad.

AS THE SAYING GOES

Trust in God but tie up your camel.

Old Persian saying

AS THE SAYING GOES

Sinning is ignorance.
If we knew enough we'd never do it.

AS THE SAYING GOES

Humankind has one main problem, we've turned our backs on God and until we turn and face Him our plight will continue to worsen.

He's not going to go away.

AS THE SAYING GOES

The less people have got
the more of it they'll give.

AS THE SAYING GOES

If all the psychologists disappeared
no one would miss them.

AS THE SAYING GOES

If we could shrink the earth's population
to a village of precisely 100,
but all existing human ratios remained
the same, it would look like this:

AS THE SAYING GOES

There would be 57 Asians, 21 Europeans,
14 Western Hemisphere people
(North and South Americas)
and 8 Africans.

continued . . .

AS THE SAYING GOES

70 of the 100 would be non-white;
30 would be white.

50 per cent of the entire world's wealth
would be in the hands of only six people –
and all six would be citizens
of the United States.

AS THE SAYING GOES

70 would be unable to read; 50 would suffer from malnutrition; 80 would live in sub-standard housing, and only one would have a university education.

(UN research via Brendan O'Sullivan)

Something not quite right there!

AS THE SAYING GOES

Listen to what someone says after they use the word "but".

AS THE SAYING GOES

If you want to get rid of someone ask them for money.

AS THE SAYING GOES

Give a young person a chance and if they respond take it to the limit. If they don't respond drop them.

AS THE SAYING GOES

If you and I conducted our affairs
like the politicians run the country
we'd be bankrupt within a year,
if not in jail.

AS THE SAYING GOES

Anyone who agrees that to pay young people the dole is a good idea is expressing a profound ignorance of human nature. If you wanted to bring a society undone without firing a shot you couldn't do better than to pay their young people to do nothing.

AS THE SAYING GOES

Men and women are equal but different, the two wings of the same bird. If one wing can't fly the bird stays grounded.

Bahai

AS THE SAYING GOES

Cliches wouldn't get to be cliches
unless they were good.

AS THE SAYING GOES

Never kick another man's dog.

AS THE SAYING GOES

Only apologise for a thing once.

AS THE SAYING GOES

No one ever regretted keeping their mouth shut when they're undecided whether to speak or not.

AS THE SAYING GOES

Like seeketh like and taketh pleasure in the company of its kind.

Bahai

AS THE SAYING GOES

Unpunctuality is bad manners.

AS THE SAYING GOES

It's more important to educate your daughter than your son.

AS THE SAYING GOES

There's no one better to be in the company of than someone who's enjoying themselves.

AS THE SAYING GOES

A bushman can adjust to the city a lot easier than a city person can adjust to the bush.

AS THE SAYING GOES

No one who fails to take care of the poor, the disadvantaged and the handicapped amongst us has any right to vaunt themselves as a leader.

AS THE SAYING GOES

You can only understand as much about other people as you understand about yourself.

AS THE SAYING GOES

Crump (to nine-year-old Kashmiri boy): "What you reckon about God, Sheffy?"

Sheffy: "God say man go in mud, man say okay!"

☙

AS THE SAYING GOES

If we concentrate on our similarities rather than our differences, we can easily see how much the same people all over the world are and the Oneness of humanity becomes conceivable.